No Failure P Training

Say Bye-Bye to Disposable Baby

Diapers with Effective Potty Training

Strategies

Leslie T. Flores

ISBN: 978-1-63750-226-6

Table of Contents

Introduction

With age-appropriate strategies for dealing with daily potty struggles and illustrations that will help you explain and teach these concepts to your child, This book shows you how to cultivate healthy emotional and intellectual development skills for potty training, so that your children can lead balanced, meaningful, and connected lives independently.

Potty training doesn't necessarily need to be hard. This Potty Training book makes it easy to get your child to start using the toilet fast and naturally because it's filled with expert advice accrued over tens of thousands cases, which has instructions with practical real life experience and advice to take you through the process of preparing child for potty training.

This Potty training book is designed to help your children

learn how to use the toilet bowl with confidence, keeping them secured and comfortable. The Author is a perfect potty trainer for little boys and girls in lavatory.

It's an erudite, resourceful, and potty book filled with fresh ideas based on the latest toilet/potty training research. I urge all parents who want kind, happy, and emotionally healthy kids to read this book. it is my new baby gift.

A useful potty training with child-friendly approach for loving parents. — Rick Reviews

Chapter 1

What to know about Potty Training

At the beginning of the grand experience of teaching a child to use the potty, many parents question how they'll ever accomplish such a complicated task. They watch their toddler with his brand-new potty dish on his head playing and questioning the sanity that persuaded them as a parent to buy the potty initially. The glad tidings are that almost all children can get better at daytime toilet/potty training at age three (3) to five (5) roughly, and for some families, it's a pleasant, even fun experience. Take the time to think about how exactly you teach your son or daughter another new lease of life skills. How will you teach your son or daughter to recite the alphabet, draw a picture, tie up his or her shoelace, dress him or herself, or come up with a puzzle?

Do you spend one full day on extreme non-formal lessons or teaching for your kids and then expect your son or daughter to pass the test by the end of the day? Would you demand that he or she show mastery every day after that without ever making any errors?

I question it! If you do approach lessons in this manner, you'd likely finish up frustrated as well as your child would maintain tears.

The actual way that people teach children new skills is by carrying it out gradually, over days, weeks, celebrating every little victory that follows. This won't apply merely to toddlers, it's a design you'll follow as an adult for quite some time too, which include your son or daughter; from the first new experience on riding bicycle, to the very first time on skis, to the new level of driving a car, and in regards to a million other new things we all do.

Considering your part in your son or daughter's learning processes, how will you strategize when teaching your son or daughter something new?

Are you going to be extreme and psychological?

Would you demand that he sit down still and give consideration?

Would you put a crayon in his hands and demand that he start painting when you sit down and get worried that he'll never figure out how to draw a compelling picture or print a capital A?

Would you consider yourself seated next to him, taking records when he would get to a better level?

Would you fret that he'll be putting on Velcro sneakers to senior high school or you need to button his tux for him on his big day?

Obviously not! You understand that your son or daughter will get good at these skills and many more during his or her lifetime, which teaching him or her is one of your jobs as a mother or father.

Think about your expectations when teaching your son or daughter something new. When teaching him to draw an image of the family, what do you anticipate to be the very first thing he'll deposit on paper? A family group portrait? No, it's a scribble! And you will take pleasure in his work and post his artwork on the refrigerator door. As time passes, and with repetition, that scribble will need shape till your son or daughter will pull circles and squares and soon homes, people, and pets.

Now let look at this next new event in your son or daughter's life: *Potty/Toilet training.* You should be able to strategize potty training in the same manner that you do every other new skill step-by-step, as time passes, with pleasure, kindness, and endurance. Let discuss those essential strategies needed to ensure smooth potty training.

When to Start Out

You can start potty training a kid at any age: you can even set a new baby on the potty bowl. However, *the most crucial question is; when will the training be finished?* A kid will complete potty/toilet training when his biology, skills, and development have matured to a spot that he's able and willing to dominate complete control of his toileting. Only then can he or she recognizes the necessity to stop his or her game, go directly to the toilet, handle the whole process, and go back to his or her game.

The quantity of time it requires for your son or daughter to understand toilet training is closely related to the span between your commencement of the training and the strategies applied; few months old when you begin training and when he or she is physically and emotionally in a position to take responsibility. Several studies also show that no matter when the potty or toilet training starts, nearly all children are just physically endowed with the capacity of 3rd party toileting after age group two, and mastery usually happens between age range two (2) and four (4).

Ensure Things are in Order

Not only will it be that you don't need to hurry the procedure, simply because rushing things can result into disaster. It places incredible stress on both you and your child. It makes the complete process a miserable experience rather than the normal learning process that it ought to be. A lot more, when stress and pressure enter the picture, it can create tantrums, constipation, extreme mishaps, and setbacks.

Your son or daughter will figure out how to use the toilet. She'll learn best in her own way and on her behalf own time plan. There is absolutely no award for the most quickly trained child. And research proves again that early or past due toileting mastery has nothing at all whatsoever regarding how smart or intelligent a kid is. So relax and revel in the process.

Can You Starting Before Child's Readiness?

A kid can be placed on the toilet bowl even while still a child, and in a few cultures this is routinely done. A little percentage of American and Canadian parents have followed this practice, called EC. Before you subscribe to thinking your daily life just got a lot easier, you should know that EC is not toilet training. It really is a long-lasting, soft, gradual system that can be used rather than diapers to control a child's waste materials. It replaces hourly diaper changes with hourly trips to the toilet.

With this technique, parents read their baby's body language and sound cues to put her on the toilet container when they believe that it is time on her behalf to defecate. The mother or father manages the child's defecation process before child is literally mature with the capacity of total individual toileting which often happens at the age range mentioned previously: from two to four years old.

If the thought of changing diapers with the strategy of watching your son or daughter's body signals and putting him or her on the potty suits you, then research one of the numerous books on this issue known as infant toilet training. In this toilet training book, we'll strategize toilet training from the more prevalent toddler-readiness approach.

Can You Get it Done in a Day?

For the vast majority of families who consider toilet training a toddler event, some can look for a fast-fix solution. However, even those interesting books or programs that guarantee one-day results have a significant stipulation: they recommend using the ideas only once a kid shows all the symptoms of readiness and reaches a starting age group of about 2yrs. In addition, they warn that bad incidents might occur for weeks afterward and the mother or father must be diligent to keep taking the kid to the toilet on a regular basis.

Basic Essentials for Potty Training a Child

There can be an enormous market for potty training paraphernalia, such as expensive dolls that soak and wet, specially made toilet chair, tot-sized urinals, fancy charts, posters, prizes, and awards. While many of these can easily make for a great experience, it isn't in any way necessary to buy a range of products for such a very simple, natural process.

A potty chair, twelve pairs of training jeans, and a relaxed and enjoyable ambiance of learning are what's needful to teach your son or daughter how to use the toilet or potty. Anything extra is optional.

Can Potty Training Decisions be made by a Child?

When deciding when to begin potty training, you will certainly want to think about your child's readiness and interest. However, if you wait around until that magic day whenever your child approaches you with a formal demand to begin potty training, you might be waiting for a very long time. A kid simply doesn't understand the worthiness of moving out of diapers to toilet independence. A kid doesn't have the knowledge, wisdom, references, or intelligence to make this kind of decision by him or herself.

Let's consider these;

Do you let your son or daughter decide his own bedtime?

Do you let him take the on business lead when he'll dress

himself? Do you want to allow him to choose when he's

prepared to begin kindergarten?

Your son or daughter counts on you to make many decisions for him or her. Despite the fact that he'd prefer to go to sleep at 10 p.m., you will decide whenever he's exhausted and yawning at 7 p.m. that is clearly a much better choice. And while he or she may want to get on the school bus along with his old brother, you understand that he's nowhere near ready for school.

Among your important assignments as a mother or father is to make decisions for your son or daughter until he or she actually is ready to make some of these trivial decisions on his or her own. With regards to potty or toilet training, she needs you to observe her for readiness cues and sunsequently apply this book ideas and strategies to her when you are feeling she's prepared to accept it and be potty trained. And you also are very experienced to get this done, because you almost certainly know your son or daughter much better than she understands herself.

Parenting Factor for Potty Decisions

Toilet/potty training isn't just an all or nothing decision. Many parents start the procedure early with the youngster because they might instead assist, remind, and tidy up a few mishaps than continue steadily to change diapers. Some decide to begin by slowly watching their child's body signals to advance to each new level. Others concentrate intently on strategies with expectations to make things work swiftly.

Any path you select for your baby can work, as long as you are positive and patient. Regardless of your plan, it can help to go from diapers to total self-reliance. For most parents, halfway is not a bad spot to be, even if indeed they spend half a year at that midpoint.

Parenting is filled up with choices, and the ultimate decisions are incredibly different for each family. There is not just one single right to toilet train or potty train a child; the methods are extensive. The right strategy for you is the one that feels convenient to you and works for you as well as your child. Eventually, you will have to assess what your loved one's goals are and then arranged an idea that is most effective for you.

How Long it Takes a Child to Learn

When toilet/potty training starts at about age group two, it can take from three (3) months to a year of toilet training before the child gains potty independence. Generally, the younger the kid is, the fewer readiness skill she possesses; the greater a mother or father must be engaged, and the much longer chance of success would take.

Regardless of your method of toilet training, 98% of children are completely independent by age four. (Nighttime dryness is another issue, predicated on physiology, and may take a lot longer.)

Potty Training and Potty Learning

The conditions *potty training* and *toilet training* have been around for decades and will be the conditions that a lot of people use to spell out the procedure. However, it isn't really about training at all, it is approximately **teaching and learning**. So; a far more accurate label for the procedure would be toilet learning or toilet teaching. With this thought, I polled more than 250 (two hundred and fifty) parents about their selection of conditions. While most of them decided it is actually about learning, 95% were sensed to be convenient with the traditional methodology and said that if indeed they were searching for a reserve on this issue, they might search the normal phrases. So, throughout this reserve, I'll stick to the time honored conditions of toilet training and potty training but as you and I both know, it's a teaching/learning process.

Helpful Facts about Potty Training

You probably don't believe much about your potty process, and it's probably so because the color and uniformity of your son or daughter's diaper deposits have been part of your daily activities. There are a few facts that are beneficial to know as you attempt the potty/toilet training journey.

- Potty training has nothing in connection with nighttime dryness. Nighttime dryness is achieved only once a child's physiology facilitates it. A kid bed-wets while asleep due to some amount of reasons: his kidneys aren't sending a sign to his brain when he's asleep to alert him he must go pee or poo, his bladder hasn't yet grown large enough to accommodate urine all night, his bladder overproduces urine at night time, or he sleeps so deeply that he doesn't stay awake to visit the toilet. As children develop, many of these conditions are personally corrected. This usually occurs between the age range of three (3) and six (6). This is not something you can educate, and you can't rush it.

- *A parent's readiness to teach is as crucial as a child's readiness to learn.* A kid can't understand how to use the toilet unless someone shows him or her. As well as the teacher's strategy and attitude can have a direct impact on how long the procedure takes and exactly how pleasurable the journey would be. A parent who is stressed about the process or who's too busy to dedicate enough time necessary for teaching can gradually complicate the procedure, or even take it to a screeching halt. Conversely, an educated, patient mother or father with a pleasurable strategy can make the process pleasurable and bring far better, and quicker result.

- Most toddlers urinate four to eight times every day, usually about every two hours roughly. A child's bladder can hold one and a half ounces of urine for every year old. (A two-year-old's bladder can take about 2-3 ounces; a three-year-old's, around 3 to 4.5 ounces; and a four-year-old's, about 4-6 ounces-less when compared to a cup.)

- Most toddlers have a couple of bowel patterns every day; some have three, while others neglect a day or two among patterns. Generally, each young one has a regular pattern.

- A child's diet will influence the total amount and frequency of urination and bowel motions. Adequate daily liquids, including drinking water, plus a nutritious diet comprising foods with a lot of fiber (fruits, vegetables, and wholegrain) can make reduction easier, which subsequently makes toilet training more comfortable.

- Ample daily exercise means that your son or daughter's stool is shifted through her system correctly. Insufficient movement can lead to constipation.

- A child's pelvic and sphincter muscles need to relax to be able to release a pee or poop. Stress, pressure, or panic is a surefire way to avoid the procedure. (That is why some children use their diaper soon after they are coming out of the toilet.).

- Polls show that more than 80 percent of parent say that their children experience some set back in toilet training. This high number indicates that what we often label as "setbacks" is just the most common way to mastery of toileting. Exactly like any new thing that children learn, it isn't always a smooth process from beginning to end. It's similar to a squiggly range, with bursts of success as well as nags and pauses on the way to the ultimate result.

- It doesn't seem to really matter what strategy can be used for toilet teaching/potty training, because 98% of children are entirely time-independent at age group four (4).

CHAPTER 2

Pre-Potty Training

When kids learn a new skill, they rarely learn it all at one time. Typically, they process the information in manageable pieces. You have to believe and understand how your son or daughter learn to process and respond to information. The process began in the past when he was a child and learned to carry up his mind and shoulders and also to control his body. He progressed to sitting down, after that to crawling, and to walking while you hold him by hand. Shortly he was cruising the home furniture. After a period, he took those initial shaky steps, as soon as those were perfected, he began to walk. This organic sequence of occasions took from ten to twenty weeks.

Just as that you patiently and methodically helped your son or daughter learn to do things naturally, you can motivate him to understand the countless details involved in potty training before you actively start potty training, that can do a lot of things that set your son or daughter up for catching up with the learning process when it's high time.

Identify the Potty Process

Each time you change your son or daughter's diaper, you have an opportunity to train a bit about elimination. Making casual comments about elimination is an excellent method to teach. Take for instance, *"You have poopoo in your diaper."* Or, *"Your diaper is wet because you peed. Mommy pees in the potty."*

A few brief explanations as time passes are helpful. You can clarify that the wetness is pee-pee and the dark brown stuff is poopoo. Inform him or her that they are leftovers that her body doesn't need. Explain a clean, dried out diaper is a lot nicer to wear.

Help your child recognize what's taking place when you see that she's wetting or filling her diaper:

Luckily for you, if you capture her tinkling in the toilet bowl or if you feel that unexpected warmth in her diaper while carrying her. At this period you can explain what she's carrying out and let her understand that in a period like that she'll learn to perform it in the potty.

Keep the Training Natural

Babies and also toddlers accept things that happen in their diaper as normal and natural. It is not until siblings, peers, and adults instruct them there's some factor disgusting about these procedures that they think in another case. Try to let your son or daughter maintain this innocent view-point about elimination. This can help toilet teaching, and potty training becomes a more definite knowledge without any embarrassment or shame. Don't attach negative worth to wet or messy diapers. (Ensure you avoid words like miserable, icky, stinky or smelly) Do not make a significant creation about the smell or consistency, and do your very best to caution your son or daughter's big brothers and sisters about this!

Teaching the Vocabulary

Throughout your everyday events, coach your toddler, the phrases and meanings of toilet-related terminologies such as body parts, urination, bowel motions, and toilet duties. When enough time comes for real potty schooling, there is so very much to learn, so that it will be useful if he or she currently is more comfortable with the necessary information.

Lots of terms that are used during potty training aren't directly toilet-related but can make different concepts for your son or daughter to comprehend. Descriptive words that you'll use during the procedure are those like wet, dry, clean, flush, and toilet paper (tissue paper).

Teach your child the idea of opposites and specific purposes which will give a foundation for toilet training. Wet/dried out, on/off, messy/clean, up/down, stop/proceed, now/later, these are concepts that'll be part of the potty training routine.

It's common for parents to employ a mixture of phrases and terms during the potty process, but doing this can confuse a fresh trainee. If for instance, you question him if he would "go potty," however, the next day you asked him "to go use the toilet," and later consult him if he must "tinkle," he might not follow your school of thought.

It is best if you choose your vocabulary conditions and adhere to them during the training process.

Importance of Reading to Your Todller

Most kids enjoy books and like to be read to. Many great children's books, created precisely for toddlers, can be found on potty training. Make an effort to get those books which have photographs of kids with books that make use of colorful pictures of pets and likely creatures learning how exactly to use the toilet.

Reading these books before training can help your son or daughter become familiar with the theory in a fun, non-threatening way without expectations attached. You can even make use of these same books as potty-time reading when teaching begins.

Carefully Select Your Potty Words!

Certain words are normal in particular geographic areas, plus some are more trusted than others. If you pay attention to daycare, the recreation center, or the retail shopping center, you'll soon know very well what words are normally used in town.

Here are a few of the words most used by families with small children:

Body Terms: Urination, bowel movement, vulva (everything you can see) and vagina (the canal inside), penis, buttocks/rectum, flatulence.

Family Words: Toilet, pot, potty, privy, loo pee, pee-pee, move potty, go pee-pee, tinkle, pissy, wee-wee, go wee, wee, wees, tee-tee, visit the bathroom, visit the toilet, utilize the potty, go (as in, "will you go?") poop, poopie, poo-poo, poos, caca, BM, move poo-poo, number two, utilize the potty, vulva, vagina, privates, bottom level, girl parts, penis, willy bottom level, bum, tush, toches/tucks, cheeks, fanny, behind, buns, rear gas, passing gas, passing wind, fart*, toot, breaking wind, blow off, poot, fluffer, stinker, etc. are regarded a rude term for children in a few families but regular in others.

Certain scientific or specialized terminologies sound odd when used with a kid. Can you envisage yourself asking your baby, "Have you got pressure in your rectum indicating that you need to defecate?" Instead, choose words that you'd be comfortable having your son or daughter use and understand fast. Use whatever phrases with which your loved ones is preferred and familiar; remember that these words will likely be called or used by your child in a general public place, so it is safer to adhere to socially acceptable language.

The Worthiness of Demonstrations

It can be beneficial to let your child see you or her siblings utilize the toilet. You won't need to have her view every detail; it's much enough to have her discover you take a seat on the toilet bowl while you explain what you are doing. Tell her that whenever she gets heavily pressed, she'll place her pee-pee and poo-poo in the toilet, too, rather than in her diaper.

If your son or daughter has older siblings, cousins, or friends, tell her that they used diapers when they were her age, however now they utilize the toilet. If they're available to accompany in the toilet, let your baby get a glimpse of his or her sibling or peer using the potty. Allow her understand that when she gets just a little older, she'll produce that act, too.

Don't assume all parent is ready to have little eye viewing while they utilize the toilet, and it's not essential for you to do that. If you like your privacy, after that teach your son or daughter to respect a shut bathroom and toilet door. Remember that as your son or daughter masters her very own toileting, she is more likely to stick to in your footsteps and desire her personal privacy as well. Set up the toilet so that it's safe and sound and manageable on her behalf, and keep hearing open when she actually is alone in the toilet.

Boost Your Son or Daughter's Independence

This is the time to encourage your son or daughter to do things on her behalf, for example; putting on her socks, draw up her pants, remove her jacket, carry a plate to the desk, and climb directly into her car seat. All of these tasks nurture a sense of independence, which will be essential for potty mastery.

As your son or daughter masters each task, her degree of confidence will develop. The more she can perform, the more she'll be ready to try. Each achievement builds on previous successes, as well as your child will discover herself to be someone who can try brand new things and be proficient at performing them. This attitude will become especially helpful when it's to introduce potty training.

Understanding How to Follow Instructions

When you begin active potty training, your child would want to know how exactly to adhere to your instructions. "Enter into the toilet." "Pull down your slacks." "Take a seat on the potty." The set of instructions will end up being long.

Start now giving your son or daughter simple directions and supporting him follow them. Request him to place a toy in the toy package. Ask her to place the glass in the sink.

At first you will have to do a large amount of prompting and reminding. You may have to move with her to greatly help her perform your request. As time passes, she'll begin to accomplish things on her very own. When she does, praise her and encourage her with hugs and kisses. Let her understand you're pleased with her being a wonderful girl.

Helping your child to understand and stick to directions are important steps essential for successful toilet and potty training.

When Should You Buy a Potty Seat?

Some parents prefer to wait to buy a potty chair until active training begins, since the appearance of a brand fresh object usually causes a spike in interest. Others prefer to get a potty and place it in the toilet a few months in advance to get their child familiar with it. If you elect to obtain a potty seat before schooling begins, you might want to present it to your son or daughter with an enthusiastic tone of voice and allow her take a seat on it. Allow her to consider the pieces aside and open up and shut the lid, if it offers one.

When you get this fresh item home, speak to your child on its purpose. You can also invite your son or daughter to take a seat on her potty by using the big toilet. You can keep it in the toilet for a couple weeks or even more to let your son or daughter get utilized to the idea prior to the teaching process commencement.

If you opt to wait until teaching commences, ensure that you choose the potty and take it out from the box and place it jointly before presenting it to your son or daughter.

Materials Necessary for Potty Training

You need to have all you need at hand before starting the potty teaching process. The information below would help you make your grocery list for potty training process.

A Portable Potty Seat

No matter what sort of toilet arrangement you possess at home, it's likely that your son or daughter will end up being facing a different circumstance when he or she's away. It's beneficial to purchase a chair adjuster that you could retain in your purse or diaper handbag. Which is a folding you can use when you're abroad. It adapts larger toilets to your son or daughter's size and makes them a bit more familiar, which is usually essential for brand-new trainees who are convenience-able with just a little potty in the home but could be overwhelmed or frightened by a large toilet and stall in an open public place.

It's wise to apply this lightweight adjuster in the home a few moments before going out. Otherwise, it's as unfamiliar as the unusual toilet you are putting it upon.

A Potty Seat or Potty Chair

A normal adult toilet doesn't fit a kid very well. It's hard to climb up to it, and a child must balance and hold himself up while seated, making elimination more challenging. The hole usually is large enough for a tyke to fall through into the water, which may be a frightening encounter for a child. An improved choice for a fresh trainee can be a child-sized potty or an adapter potty chair insert along with a sturdy footstool.

There are many types available, so check around online store. A child-sized seat or chair is certainly essential to help significantly provide the toilet right down to your son or daughter's size and make it friendly, secure, and manageable. Almost any type will work, and the decision is yours.

Some potty seats have a high, removable splash safeguard created to prevent a fresh trainee from splattering the toilet. While the purpose for these is ordinarily useful plus they can serve the reason, splash guards also present a personal injury hazard. Many kids lose their balance in the process.

Decide Where You Can Put The Potty

If you are utilizing a potty chair rather than an insert, you can stick it wherever you would like. Many households place the potty in the toilet right beside the big toilet. The benefit to this is that your son or daughter gets accustomed to the location, and it creates access for easy dumping and washing. It also helps a kid connect the potty with the actions that follow because other members of the family use the toilet in the same space.

The disadvantage to maintaining your child's potty close to the toilet is that if your toilet is quite a few distances away from the places in your house where your son or daughter spends his or her time, you might have several accidents initially while he or she is on the path to the toilet. This will stop, however, as your son or daughter gets utilized to reading his body signs.

Some families decide to keep the potty seat in the area where the kid spends time mostly. Throughout the day, it could be kept in your lobby. If you do that, it's wise to create a small potty nook or part to permit a child, therefore, have privacy and to reinforce the idea that this is not a public event. Through the bedtime routine and overnight, the potty could be kept in the bedroom for easy access, if you'd like. The benefit of a portable potty is definitely that your son or daughter is most likely to access the potty in time. The drawback is definitely that at some time, you will have to transfer your son or daughter's urine or feces to the toilet, but most children get this to change easily after they are potty trained.

Training Pants

Get a way to obtain a dozen or even more cotton training pants or a few boxes of disposable pull-up trousers.

These will herald the brand new stage of advancement for your child and become a clear transmission that something fresh has begun.

Thick absorbent training jeans (instead of regular underwear) are excellent for new trainees. They'll absorb most or all your child's accidents and protect your floors and furniture.

Disposable pull-up pants are a well-known choice for brand-new trainees. Take note, however, that the disposables can backfire (as they say). Because they may feel like diapers to your child, your child may deal with them as such. Consider among the new types that certainly are a little much less unwieldy and also have an obtain-wet liner which allows your son or daughter to feel the wetness, which can only help him to recognize, and ideally avoid wet sense.

Children can change to less bulky and more attractive underwear after they start to show some improvement.

Chapter 3

Factors to Consider When Buying Potty Chair/Seat

Toilet Seat Adapter (Adapter Potty Seat)

Pros :

- The child does not have to adjust from a kid seat to an adult toilet.

- You won't have a potty chair on your own bathroom floor.

- There is absolutely no potty seat bowl to completely clean out.

Cons:

- It isn't child-sized.

- The kid must use excrement or get an adult's help to climb up.

- The child's foot will dangle, so a footstool (where the child can place his or her feet) is essential.

- Adults must cope with the insert if they want to use the toilet.

- The child should be supervised by a grown-up throughout all uses.

- You need to purchase one for every toilet or move it from one toilet to another.

Adult Toilet Seat

Pros:

- There is absolutely no learning adjustment from chair to seat.

- The child may use any toilet once he learns to utilize the one at home.

Cons:

- It isn't as enticing to a kid as a colorful child's potty chair.

- It really is oversized for a kid, which may be intimidating.

- The kid might fall off the chair or into the water.

- The kid will require a footstool to plant feet.

- The child should be supervised by a grown-up throughout all uses.

Free-standing Potty Chair

Pros :

- It is little in size, simple to use, and non-threatening.

- It really is designed particularly for a child's little

body.

- It enables the kid to plant his feet on the floor.

- It comes in bright shades and child-friendly designs.

- It is portable such that can be moved around.

- It promotes independence as it could be utilized by a child on his or her own.

Cons :

- The bowl should be cleaned out after every use.

- The child will need to transit to a normal toilet later.

- The kid may still want a toilet seat when moving up to the big toilet.

- When you are abroad or away from home, you need to bring the potty or your son or daughter must adjust to the distinctions in equipment available.

- Portability makes it too much such as a toy (leaving it open to misuse).

- You need to purchase one for every toilet or move it from one toilet to another.

Potty Chair Buying Checklist

i. The seat size fits the child's body size.

ii. The splash guard is low, padded, or removable.

iii. The bottom is steady and sturdy.

iv. The bowl is simple to remove for cleaning.

v. The seat is comfortable, perhaps cushioned.

vi. It really is portable for shifting from place to place or for trip away from home.

vii. It comes with an appealing style.

viii.   It has great functionality.

Climbing over and falling could easily get a child bruised in an exceedingly delicate region when climbing on or off the potty. Either of the situations could cause a concern with the potty and develop a major setback. It's easier to teach your small boy to carry his penis right down to pee and your little lady to rest and lean ahead a bit, rather than backward, that will prevent any splashing. If you choose to use an insert that suits in to the regular toilet, you will have to get one to suit your toilet chair, which may be circular or elongated. Additionally, you will need excrement. This serves two purposes for your child to climb up to the chair and to make use of it as a system for his or her footstool. It really is much harder to regulate the sphincter muscle groups when foot are dangling in the atmosphere.

If your son or daughter spends an amount of time in two different homes, or if the toilets in your house are far aside from each other, buy many of the same potty to keep things easy and consistent.

Think about your child's personality before purchasing a potty for him or her.

Do you consider that your child will become more accepting of the potty if he or she accompanies you to the shop to choose it out?

If therefore, go on and shop collectively. Take one from the container and let him or her take a seat on it in the shop. Or simply make your child want it better in the event that you covered it up in a colourful wrapping paper and show it to him or her as a surprise. Either choice is okay.

Potty Training Tricks and Treats

Plenty of interesting accessories are for sale for potty training such as: musical potty chair, bull's-attention grabbber, toddler- sized urinals, dissolving floaters, dolls, and prize charts are a few examples. None of these are essential, but lots of them are fun, and therefore can motivate your kid and move the procedure happily along. Choose your tips thoughtfully, mainly because some can even be more of a distraction rather than help. Many parents explained using musical enabled potties to having their kids leap up midstream and eventually see the potty event as fun.

If something catches your eye and you imagine it, this will make the procedure more fun for your son or daughter, go ahead and check it out.

CHAPTER 4

Elimination Communication

Elimination Communication is the practice that involves making use of your child's cues to greatly help them get rid of their waste. For some, it appears like zero diaper use ever, while for others, it's a mixture of using diapers. It doesn't actually matter how long you've used EC or how regular.

Now, you're scanning this, which means no matter current EC literature, you understand in your heart, it's sure for completion. I'm likely to call this completion procedure a "bridge," for brevity; a bridge from there to here.

I actually contacted some EC specialists because increasingly more people wish to potty train before twenty weeks. I completely support this but discovered this might be a particular percentage of Elimination Communication and a specific percentage of Potty training.

However, below are several things that are part of EC that may make potty training a little difficult.

1. Diaper-free Time.

2. Getting the pee, not shifting to the potty.

3. Philosophy.

4. The idea that your son or daughter will simply potty train themselves.

5. The expectation that EC offers you a joint potty training.

6. Potty strike.

Diaper-free Time

We don't know about your position but also for many

parents, Diaper-free Period gets misconstrued. For most, Diaper-free time probably condition your son or daughter to pee on to the floor.

I've heard many tales of children who just stay naked all day long with parents attempting catches but really just clearing up a whole lot of pee. I talked to numerous EC experts over time. I couldn't wrap my head for this particular practice.

There's just therefore much to learn that every moment can be an experiment and discovery. So if they pour their milk away on the ground, it's for the pleasure of viewing, "Oh . . . this occurs when I do that. Great."

Nevertheless, it's our work as parents to tell them that pouring milk on the floor isn't suitable. While we wouldn't yell or shame them, we'd consistently most likely frown and say something comparable to, "No, no . . . zero milk stays up for grabs."

So, now let's consider the cause and after-effect of peeing anywhere, anytime the desire hits. If you never let your kid know that it's unacceptable, you won't like the aftermath effect. It's consequently learned behavior to simply pee where you have to pee. This may be okay in the first days, whatever age group you started elimination communication, but once your child regularly does this for just about any big chunk of period, it's kind of cemented in. In other terms, you've traded a diaper for your floor.

The only reason I talk about Diaper-free Time is since the initial thing I hear from an EC Mama is level of resistance to a naked day time.

The naked day time is quite crucial to one of the largest steps in building the bridge from EC to PT, which lead us to issue number 2.

Getting Pee, and not on a Potty

So far in EC, you almost certainly have an incredible bond with your child. You understand her signals and you hurry to take her potty, mostly where it's convenient. I really like the actual fact that EC offers you "permission" to potty anywhere. Nevertheless, once you officially begin potty schooling, you do need to get your son or daughter to the potty of choice (either the tiny potty or the place on the toilet). The big thing here's getting the child physically to the correct place. However, the norm is to be getting the kid to the potty. I'd say this task alone may be the biggest in the bridge from there to here.

Philosophy

I understand that "traditional potty schooling" is a dirty term in EC. I understand there are "shoe camps" for potty training and all types of coercive methods or advice. However, at times I discover myself having to remind parents that it's alright to possess boundaries and objectives. There's a whole lot of philosophy around

EC and attaching parenting that sometimes falls aside as your son or daughter nears the twos. I don't think the twos have to be terrible by any stretch, nevertheless, you may find that a few of this EC-associated philosophy doesn't endure. I don't wish to argue this aspect, and I'm not really saying anything about anyone's parenting design. I just find this as certainly a difficult place in parenting to keep up theory. Your child will begin limit screening, and his favourite word is going to be "No."

Most of the philosophy suggests that there may be nothing bad around the potty.

Very much as in the "milk on to the floor" cause-and-effect example, you do need to tell your son or daughter what your positive expectation is and what the adverse expectation is. This doesn't have to sound mean, but you do have to mean business. At some time your child must find out that peeing simply anywhere is a "don't." A lot of parents emphasize the positive end of issues ("just pee in the potty"), but they omit the other section of the equation ("don't pee somewhere else"). Therefore, yes, you definitely want to emphasize the positive, but be sure you are getting clear in what you don't need as well.

Expecting Your Toddler to Potty Teach Him or Herself

Occasionally a child will opt to potty himself. Generally, this is simply not the case, however, which makes feeling if you think about any of it. And that's most likely why you are right here. Peeing and pooping are primal behaviors, do you agree? You don't need to teach a child how exactly to pee or poop. Placing it in a container of some kind is a socialized behavior. Socialized behavior should be taught, the simplest way to obtain it is to slap it all out of your hands. That's primal. The socialized way of setting it up is to ask or negotiate. That's what should be taught.

How do we train that?

When our kids utilize the primal instinct to slap something out of someone's hand, we gaze at them in the eye, we say in a fairly stern voice, "Zero hitting. You ask." We most likely frown or make a disapproving facial expression. We are far better whenever we use simple vocabulary. "No this, Yes that." There doesn't have to be a ton of discussion about this. I think most of us, as a whole are doing a significant amount of talking. I specifically think that is true in potty teaching. It's similar to your son or daughter learning the ABCs. They aren't learning all of the power behind the letters that produce different sounds at differing times in an incredible number of combinations. In potty training, the brief, more direct words function best.

The Expectation That Elimination Communication Offers You Potty Training

I believe bridging EC with PT is the hardest part with respect to coping with the expectation that because you've been functioning at this for a reasonably long time, this will become easy for your son or daughter. Trust me, I think this will be true as well. I don't desire you to end up being mad at me, but I've discovered that this isn't necessarily the case. It's a genuine freaking bummer.

And the actual fact that you're most likely not to get one is actually hard to wrap your mind around. What I've found is that once you're more than the hump, ECed children tend to move considerably faster and the training "sticks" far better. And you possess the bonus of not just a great relationship but also of understanding your child's signals.

What I've found is most effective for ECers who wish to potty teach is to simply consider this as another (separate) process. Your son or daughter most likely hasn't made the bond that she is normally the main one who should be in action after the feeling of experiencing to pee strikes. As well as your child is probably extremely used to peeing as the urge hits. It's the slightest adjustment which will make this much easier. Another pitfall is whenever your child is definitely taking longer than typical.

CHAPTER 5

Potty Training Your Child

Having decided that the time is here to commence potty and toilet training, your son or daughter is ready and you're prepared. So, what's next?

Firstly, ensure that your attitude and expectations are in the best place. You ought to be feeling calm and positive. It's also advisable to understand that the training process may take as long as half a year or more, so forget about any hope you may have to toilet train your toddler in merely a day. Exactly like learning how to walk, chat, or take beverage from a cup, understanding how to utilize the toilet bowl, and really should end up being a gradual, pleasurable experience for you both.

Before you place a potty in the toilet, it is time to create your supplies and execute a little planning. Below are the necessary measures to take.

Forming Your Potty-Training Strategy

There isn't just one single best way to potty train a child. There are various approaches that can lead you to success. As you make decisions about how exactly to begin this grand endeavor, have a few things to consider:

- What is your son or daughter's learning design? How has he or she learned various other new skills? Will he or she observe and absorb before she tackles something? Or will he or she dive in and function her method through it? Is he or she a thoughtful listener or a hands-on doer?

- What exactly do you do that mostly motivates him or her to try something new? What activities bring the best outcomes? Is your enthusiasm more than enough to get your child to try something new? Or what activities do you perform to convince and persuade him or her before he or she will test it out? Will he or she do anything his or her old sibling or cousin will?

- What's your teaching design and strategy? Do you describe verbally before you display? Do you present it step-by-step with commentary? Do you perform by gently demonstrating? Do you set items up and allow your child to find out what's happening by himself?

- How much time have you got to potty train your child? Are you available all day together with your kid or home only at a specific time of the day? Will you devote an uninterrupted chunk of the period to get started, accompanied by snippets of time each day afterward? Or are you considering fitting training into your already busy schedule?

- What are your targets? What do you consider would be much easier for you: changing diapers or assisting your son or daughter on the potty? Would you instead concentrate intently on potty schooling for two weeks and move issues along? Or do you read articles to teach and train while you let your son or daughter set the speed, mastering one stage at a time?

- Who'll be the teachers? Do you want to potty train by yourself? Or will several people be involved in the training?

Most of these issues can affect the toilet/potty training experience. Taking time to examine these points can help you plan the best strategy for you, your son or daughter, and the others of your loved ones, too.

Factors that Enhances Successful Training

Whether you are employing elimination communication with a three-month-old, pre-training an eighteen-month-old, or introducing a brand-new concept to a three-year-old, there are two important factors that may affect the process above all, both of these factors will establish the pace for potty training. These could make the toilet schooling journey a demanding, unpleasant event, or even ensure that it is an excellent, successful process.

These two factors could make your son or daughter miserable or make him or her content. They can make any strategy an unexpected disaster, or they can make nearly every potty/toilet training method work beautifully.

What exactly are these excellent factors? *The teacher's attitude and the teacher's degree of patience.*

Allow me to say this again to ensure that you grasp this essential concept. *Both factors which will set the speed for potty training effectiveness are your **attitude as well as your patience**.*

You'll remember that I didn't mention anything about the mentee or student! That's because kids learn factors from their parents and other folks in their life, which is what they practice. And kids are like small sponges. Children are continually watching others, specifically the adults in their life. They grab cues from others about how exactly they should respond in a variety of situations; whether it's the first time on an equine, the first flavor of papaya or the first take a seat on a potty chair, your child will end up being learning from you.

So, no matter where your son or daughter is in the readiness department, and regardless of what approach you choose to take, be sure that these factors are in proper place before starting potty training process.

The two important indicators for effective and successful toilet schooling process popularly known as potty training are;

   i.   The teacher's positive and supportive attitude.

   ii.   The teacher's kind and understanding tolerance.

Potty Training Methodologies

Once you've decided about how you'll approach potty training with your kid and gathered all of your supplies, it's nearly time to start the process actively. Following are a few points to consider as you progress.

Keep in mind the two miracle factors; the teacher's excellent attitude and kind patience will set the pace for the toilet or potty-training journey. Take a breath, relax, and appreciate the knowledge with your baby.

Dress Him or Her for Training Success

It's more challenging for a toddler to get to the toilet in time but having the complication of snaps, zippers, and buttons. Many a trainee managed to get to the toilet and then have a major accident standing before the toilet, wanting to undress. For another couple of months and probably actually longer, your son or daughter should, whenever possible, avoid wearing pants with buttons, snaps, belts, or zippers and T-shirts that hang beneath the waist. Be sure that your son or daughter can remove her clothes easily and quickly. Regarding dresses, get them short more than enough to be able to remove them completely and well taken care of.

The very best clothing for a fresh potty trainee is a T-shirt and shorts or slacks with an elastic waistband. Make certain these are relatively loose fit so that your son or daughter can easily have them up and down.

At the start of training, you might want to have your son or daughter actually remove his or her trousers and underwear when he or she uses the potty, because there are a great number of new things to consider and having a wad of jeans around his or her ankles could be distracting and partially lowered slacks can become splattered. If you do not have him remove his trousers, feel absolve to help him consider his clothing off and place them back on, also if he can perform it himself. Needing to dress and undress in about ten situations a day will work fast for a dynamic toddler and may result in disinterest in using the potty at all. Don't worry, though he or she will adapt to this section of the process very quickly.

Be Optimistic

Understanding how to master toileting is normally a huge task for just a little child (kids). Mastery comes into play with time and patience. Sometimes will be more effective in some children than others. Sometimes when the house is tranquil and the day to day routine is definitely in place, your son or daughter will significantly have more success.

Training Pants or Diapers Strategy

Once your child gets a general idea and has started having daily success on the potty, you might want to change from diapers or disposable pull-up to cloth teaching pants to make things go along even faster.

The drawback to thickly padded disposable diapers or

super-absorbent training pants is that they disguise wetness so very much that your son or daughter probably isn't bothered about it, whereas cotton training pants, or disposables with a stay-wet liner, signal wetness immediately and aren't extremely comfortable to wear when wet or messy. This can help your child to be more alert to what's happening down there.

Also, be sure you keep your son or daughter's pants a little loose so your baby can pull them easily. Training slacks or pull-ups ought to be a size larger than necessary. You desire them to be manageable for your son or daughter, without being so big that they droop.

Make the Process Child-Friendly

Can your child easily open the door and turn on the light? Reach the toilet paper? Get right up to the sink? If he or she is facing difficulty addressing and using her potty, she'll be less thinking about using it routinely. Also, if she counts on you to perform everything on her behalf, you'll be passing up on a wonderful facet of potty teaching: encouraging your son or daughter's independence is vital.

Many small children are suspicious of empty rooms, and several fear the dark. There is nothing scarier compared to the cavern of a dark toilet. Through the training months, and perhaps actually for an extended period after schooling, accept that you'll either need to accompany your kid each time or keep the way and toilet carefully well to chase apart any unwanted shadows.

Clothing Strategy

If you're fortunate to begin training in warm weather, or when you can turn heat up in your house during training, hold your toddler in only training pants for a week roughly. Children often resist coping with ON/OFF requirement during teaching, since it takes so very much time and effort based on their limited skills. Therefore, the less clothing to cope with, the better!

Some parents let their children roam naked during training, but it isn't for everyone. Consider it before you bring in the theory to your baby, because he or she is more likely to like the freedom and could surprise you by carrying out a bit more of it than you expect. You might want to consider your family's method of nudity. How are things managed during bath time? How can you respond if your son or daughter walks in when you are dressing? If your family culture is certainly one of modesty and you suddenly let your son or daughter roam the home naked, it could send him or her some complicated mixed messages.

However, some families are even more relaxed about your body's natural state. Kids, siblings, and parents bathe jointly, toddlers play in the toilet as Mommy showers and dresses, and little males potty trained while peeing alongside Daddy. If this describes your family style, then you might look for a small extra time to help your child tune in with her body's elimination process.

One of the various other things to take into account here is that whenever using the naked strategy, all those early mishaps (among several others) will be unhindered by clothes and property unprotected wherever your son or daughter might be, and it will not be his or her fault or whatever you can prevent. For those who have carpeting or home furniture that may be ruined by accidents, you may take working out of the backyard or choose to go the almost naked approach instead and pop a set of training jeans on your little one.

Take Things Slow

If you feel relaxed about the procedure, it's likely your son or daughter will as well. Ironically, the much less you push, the quicker the outcomes will occur.

The more you hurry, the much longer it will require. Even if a day time or an additional deadline looms, don't hurry the process with an excessive amount of strength and pressure. Being even more relaxed can help your child find out more conveniently and will get this to be less demanding for you too.

Potty Training Abroad/Far from Home

New trainees could just be getting more comfortable with the potty routine in the home but are unlikely to really have the same success in public areas or while traveling from one place to another. It could be irritating for a mother or father to have to handle repeated incidents in the automobile or while abroad or away from home. There are numerous methods to handle being abroad with a kid in training.

You can simply opt to keep your son or daughter in diapers or disposable pants when abroad. Most children very easily adjust to the idea that there exists a change into diapers or pull-ups when you go out. Create a schedule: the kid goes potty and places on pull-ups before you go out and then adjusting back to training trousers or underwear when you come back home.

Other options listed below are to put your son or daughter's diaper or pull-ups more than his training jeans or make use of a waterproof diaper cover more than his training slacks. He may experience been happier if he will keep his big boy trousers on, yet he'll experience the wetness if he comes with an accident. It's sort of a mid-step that may keep you calm in the automobile while helping him discover that he or she is growing up.

If you'd prefer never to put your son or daughter on diapers when you are away your home, ensure that you are ready to handle on-the-street potty phone calls and potty mishaps. Bring along a portable potty for use in the automobile and a folding chair adapter for use in toilets. Cover the automobile seat with plastic material, and for cleanup, provide along wet wipes, plastic material luggage, and paper towels. Prepare yourself with a complete change of clothing, and perhaps socks and shoes.

And be sure you bring your persistence and good humor, as well. You will have bad incidents, therefore accept them, clean them up, change your son or daughter's clothes, and move on.

Naps and Bedtime Method

Many children will remain in nighttime diapers for a year
or much longer after daytime achievement. Nighttime
dryness is attained only once a child's biology facilitates
this, you can't hurry it, so don't also try. (Occasional bed-
wetting is known as normal until approaching age six.)
Maintain a routine of placing diapers or disposable pull-
up on your kid for naps or bedtime. The moment he or
she is awake, remove it and also have him or her utilize
the potty because so many children will eliminate soon
after getting up. Switch your son or daughter out of night
time diapers when the morning hours diaper is regularly
dry.

Chapter 6

How to Read a Child's Body Sign for Potty Event

Understanding your child's body signal for potty activities enable you to help him or her get to the toilet fast.

The following are some typically common signals of an imminent bowel movement:

- Timing (very first thing each morning or ten to thirty minutes after a meal).

- Passing-by repeatedly.

- Squatting.

- Touching diaper.

- Tensed facial expression.

- Grunting.

- Stopping active play.

- Bending forward while holding tummy.

- Stomach-ache.

And below are a few common signals of impending urination:

- Timing (very first thing on awakening each morning or after a nap, one and half hour (1.5hrs) to two hours (2hrs) after last pee, or twenty (20) to forty-five minutes (45mins) after drinking).

- Holding crotch.

- Sitting on heels.

- Crossing legs.

- Squeezing thighs together.

- Squirming and wiggling (the potty dance).

- Bouncing.

- Shifting from feet to foot.

- Rocking backward and forwards.

- Becoming still and motionless.

- Whimpering.

The most crucial thing to bear in mind is that it is their (kids) accomplishment and milestone, not yours as a parent. **It is important to be sensitive to their timeline.**

The more we support them in having their success and their very own accomplishment (with only a small amount of psychological attachment on our side), the quicker the achievement and the more pleasant the knowledge for kids and parents!

When your child's day to day routine is disrupted or when he's overtired, hungry, or overstimulated, he'll likely have significantly more accidents and become more forgetful in what he or she is said to be doing.

Teaching your kid how to utilize the toilet is unarguably a permanent lesson. Between dried outruns and real potty calls, you will probably find yourself accompanying him to the toilet up to a dozen times a day! That results in 84 times support to the toilet over a week and some 360 times per month!

One method to keep perspective is to write down the starting day of potty teaching and note another time of about 90 days to the future. Understand that you'll end up being your kid's potty partner for at least those 90 days. Remember, it could take typically three (3) to a year of schooling until your son or daughter will be ultimately toilet independence depending on the pace of learning and teaching strategies applied by you.

CHAPTER 7

Potty Training a Boy and a Girl

In most cases it is recommended to start potty lessons with your son seated to pee. The principal reason for that is that if you train him to pee taking a stand, you'll be splitting toilet teaching into two separate stages: *urination and bowel schooling.*

How to Potty Train a Boy & a Girl

You might have heard that little male finish toilet training later than female. They do tend to have some differences; however, the quantity is insignificant in the picture as a whole. Studies show that normally, girls take about one to three months before boys, both with showing readiness abilities and with daytime and nighttime independence. Nevertheless, all children will vary, and this range for beginning and finishing training is very broad. Also, since the whole process may take up to a year from beginning to end, the difference most likely won't mean very much to your family.

Children's individual personality features, readiness factors, and age group at teaching and the parent's strategy are more significant elements in the timing of toilet training to pee, the much more likely you are to capture a poop along the way, especially because they often times occur simultaneously.

It's also practical to wait to instruct your son how precisely to stand and urinate until he's tall enough to easily master the desire to pee into the bowl. Until after that, keep your small boy on the potty seat, and get him in the habit of keeping his male organ pointed straight down toward the bowl in order to avoid having him sprinkle beyond your potty. You could also try having him sit down and straddle the toilet chair facing backward. It's less difficult for him to climb up in this manner, and it also places him in the correct position for elimination. Also, you'll avoid the overspray that may wet his clothe, the floor, the wall and you.

A fresh option is available in the market "toddler-sized urinal potties". This appears like a miniature version of a regular urinal but has a bucket just like a potty seat does. If you are using one of these, be sure you either install it on an easy-to-clean floor surface area or place a plastic mat around the base until your little boy masters his goal. The potential issue with teaching a little boy to stand to pee right away is that it could hinder bowel training. Kids must sit down and relax on the potty to be able to have a bowel motion, and because BMs frequently accompany pee, having male's potty trained while seated often produces far better and easier training.

Once your little man has begun to understand toilet training and is high enough to attain the toilet bowl very easily, you can change him to taking a stand at the standard toilet. If your kid has been more comfortable with family members nudity i.e. following family members by example during toilet time, and if Daddy or a brother is usually a willing instructor, have one of these show your child how this is done.

As the mom or dad, teach your little boy to lift the potty cover to pee and to close when done. In the event that you teach him to master this as a habit, he'll usually do it that method. Otherwise, women who utilize the toilet after your child does are certain to get the shock of seating on a splattering of urine or faeces which is very absurd.

Be Prepared to Reach a Toilet Quickly

Even before your son or daughter asks, ensure that you always know where exactly the toilet is; if you are in a shop, a friend's house, or anywhere else. In this manner, you can move quickly whenever your child announces the necessity to go pee or poo.

A child who is not used to these potty lessons might wait before last minute to announce his or her necessity to go pee or poo. Whenever your child says she's pressed, reach the potty and perform it quickly! While it's occasionally annoying to need to quit everything to consider taking him or her to the toilet, this is specifically everything you have been wishing to achieve. Your son or daughter is recognizing the desire and delaying elimination until he or she reaches the toilet. So show patience and support, even though the urgent quest may cause you to quit whatever you are doing at the moment.

Get Him or Her to Jump to Start with Indicators

If your child is worked up about potty training and seems to be getting the hang of it, or in case you have a potty dead collection you need to meet, you might help speed up the procedure.

Select a day when you'll be home all day and will have no outdoor engagement. Give your son or daughter lots of salty snack foods and juice or drinking water or beverage. Watch him or her cautiously for indicators to pee or poo, or set a timer or maintain a log to ensure that you keep in mind the approximate time to execute a potty function every 30 mins. Make an effort to think of methods to make this a great event.

The ideology is that; taking more liquid in means even more liquid out, so you should have lots of practice appointments to the toilet. And everybody knows that practice makes ideal perfection!

If your son or daughter spends time in someone else's care, make sure everyone communicates with one another relating to your child's potty teaching. Have a clear plan for potty training to ensure that everyone is constant whenever taking care of your child.

Duration of Praise and Reward Strategy

Some specialists say that you need to give a whole load of positive opinions, including a partylike atmosphere-actually with noisemakers, cake, and party hats. Others state that you ough to avoid getting overly thrilled or emotional and acknowledge that your son or daughter has done well.

The proper answer is that the proper answer is different for each parent and child pair. Some parents are naturally more thinking about everything their kids perform; others tend to be reserved.

Some women thrive on the parents' energy, other kids are easily overwhelmed. Even two different kids in the same family will respond easily to different degrees of enthusiasm.

Probably the finest advice is to accomplish what comes naturally. What's most significant is that you would like your child to learn that you support him, that you will be pleased with his efforts and also his successes.

Offer Reward to Boost Potty Learning

In case you are not certain that your son or daughter is physically ready for potty training, I'd advise against using any type of prize system. If he or she is physically unable to utilize the potty individually, you'll just be establishing him or her up for disappointment.

If, however, your child is set physically for potty schooling but is reluctant emotionally or adapting to the theory slowly, you might help spark the process with reward or "potty prizes." Regardless of what you've considered giving kids prizes as rewards previously, there are occasions to utilize this effective idea during potty teaching. According to some polls, a lot more than 80 percent of parents conforms to giving their children benefits or prizes for using the potty, so you would be in good company.

Survey has revealed that most kids and preschoolers could be highly motivated to create adjustments when offered prizes-which, I'm sure, is a great surprise for you! There are many approaches you may use.

Potty Prize Treasure Box Strategy

Many parents have reported fantastic success with this vibrant idea. Here's how it operates:

- Purchase about thirty inexpensive little prizes. (Check the toy stores for an excellent collection of inexpensive trinkets.).

- Wrap each prize separately in colorful wrapping paper.

- Place the prizes in a clear plastic bowl on the toilet counter. You can call it the Potty Prize Treasure Package, or various other fun and enticing name.

- Tell your son or daughter, "They are potty prizes.

You'll receive one every time you carry out your business in the toilet, simply with no hurry but whenever you're ready."

Most kids are "prepared" immediately, but you shouldn't be surprised if your son or daughter drools more than the prize bowl for some days before making a decision to be ready.

Allow your kid to select one prize every time he or she will go. By enough time the prize bowl is certainly empty, the habit will end up being firmly set up. If your child requests a prize following the exhausting of the Treasure Packages, inquire to find a few of his or her aged prizes and simply wrap them up once again. (Truly. The fun is normally in the unwrapping!)

After a while your son or daughter will start to forget to require a prize, and you may easily move to the "no-prize" phase.

Relax during Accidents

Accidents are likely to happen during the training period. Utilize the same approach you utilize when she buttons her sweater the wrong manner or spills some milk. *"Oops. Missed the potty at that point. Don't worry, pretty soon you'll get it right."*

Accidents are extremely normal, especially in the beginning of training. Nevertheless, if your son or daughter is having a lot more accidents than successes, or if either you or your son or daughter is getting distressed about these incidents, you might want to retake the readiness quiz to observe only if you've started a little too early.

Accidents are inevitable initially, however they should steadily decrease. If indeed they continue after your son or daughter has completed training, nevertheless, you might need to examine the reason for them. If your son or daughter is just too busy to avoid her activity to access the toilet, perhaps you're in best position to make it possible for him or her to recuperate from these episodes. You might like to get her more mixed up in cleanup process. Train your child how precisely to help clean up any mess, change his or her personal clothing, and put her filthy pants in the laundry. If she's to help you look after all of this, it could help reduce these mishaps. It's typical for a kid to master taking care of potty schooling before another, so avoid being surprised of accidents happening for some time. Just maintain praising her successful attempts and keep focusing on the less-consistent process.

Exercise Enough Patience

This whole process does take time. You almost certainly won't feel confident to completely start your son or daughter's toileting for most months. So relax, show patience, and revel in the journey. Kids are just little for an extremely short time to embrace the training effectively.

Chapter 8

Importance of Hand Cleaning During Potty Routine

Cleaning hands after using the toilet is usually a major deterrent to the pass on of germs and contamination, yet research demonstrates many adults don't routinely clean their hands after toilet appointments, and several don't do a sufficient job of washing if in any case they carry it out. While 95% of women and men surveyed say they clean their hands after utilizing a public restroom, about 50% actually do it, based on the outcomes of an observational research.

Women surveyed were considerably more likely than males to state that they clean their hands.

"Hand washing may be the simplest, most reliable thing people may do to lessen the spread of infectious dis-

eases," according to Julie Gerberding, M.D., director of a healthcare facility Infections System, Centers for Disease Control and Avoidance.

You can instill this healthy lifelong hand-washing habit in your son or daughter by building a standard section of the potty check out every time, whether he makes a deposit or not. Most children like to perform and splash water, so with just a little encouragement, your son or daughter will happily adopt this concept.

Just make sure to have a durable step stool to ensure that your child can simply reach the sink. Select colourful soaps, foam soap dispensers, or child-friendly soaps. You may even ensure to have several variations available to ensure that he or she makes a choice about which to make use of. Don't hurry the process, and make certain he or she lathers up, which may be great fun. Supervise an intensive rinsing, and also have an easy to get towel for drying off.

You can motivate your kid's independence by teaching him or her how specifically to do this alone.

CHAPTER 9

Overcoming Bed Wetting

When your son or daughter uses the toilet all day with only rare errors, you can think about your toilet training working effectively, even if your son or daughter still wears a diaper to bed. Nighttime dryness is an entirely separate subject.

Toilet schooling is accomplished whenever a child runs on the potty seat or toilet for bladder and bowel features during waking hours.

As children grow and develop, so carry out their ability to regulate their bladder. There is normally a wide variety of "normal" for whenever a kid achieves nighttime control. Bed-wetting, known as *enuresis*, is usually common amongst young children, with an increased percentage of males than girls. Because nearly half of most three-year-old's or more to 40 percent of four-year-old's wet the bed many times a week, it is considered normal behavior at these age groups. Additionally, 20 to 25 percent of five-year-old's and 10 to 15 percent of six-year-olds don't stay dry out every night.

By age nine, just 5 percent of children wet the bed, and the majority of those children do it only one time per month. As children grow older, few of them possess bed-wetting accidents. In nearly all cases, the issue goes away completely even when parents avoid any unique treatment for the problem, and with the tiny percentage of kids who do want help, treatment is not at all hard.

The most commonly known reasons for bed-wetting in a kid are because of his or her physiology. Your son or daughter's child kidney aren't sending a sign to his or her mind when asleep, the brain is as well profoundly sleeping to listen to the indicators, his or her bladder hasn't grown huge enough to include a full night's way to hold urine or his or her organ over-produces urine during the night. As kids grow, most of these conditions are self-corrected.

Bed-wetting can be hereditary, so if one or both parents had been a bed wetter, a kid has about an 80 percent chance of doing the same by bed wetting. Diabetes, food sensitivities (particularly to caffeine, milk products, fruit, and chocolate), some medications, or additional health conditions can influence nighttime bladder-control problems. On occasion, bed-wetting could be a sign of a rest disorder; therefore if your son or daughter exhibits other indications, such as snoring or restless sleep, you might want to investigate this possibility.

No kid chooses to awaken cold and wet. Bed-wetting almost never is really because a kid is lazy or disobedient. Exactly like understanding how to walk or understanding how to talk, there's an array of "normal," and, like other milestones, every child achieves nighttime dryness on his or her time schedule. There is no reason to hurry the process.

For a bed-wetting toddler or preschooler, the perfect solution is easy: *allow your son or daughter to rest for naps and evening time in a diaper, padded teaching trousers, or disposable absorbent underpants until he or she starts to remain dry during naps and forever long.*

How to know when Safe to go Diaper-less?

When your kid has been sleeping dry for a week or more,

it might be safe to get one of these night time or nap without diapers. Be ready for occasional accidents. The good idea is to double-make the bed. (Make use of a waterproof pad atop the bed sheet, and cover this with a second sheet which can be quickly removed if your son or daughter wets at night.) Keep an extra pair of pajamas nearby.

Some children appear to learn whenever a diaper is on the bottoms and utilize it rather than building a night or early-morning hours visit to the toilet. If your son or daughter is day-time independent and you imagine that she could be prepared to go without a diaper when sleeping, go ahead and test it out if she's prepared. As an experiment, make your child proceed diaper-less, sleeping atop a waterproof pad and double-made bed, to observe how he or she responds. You (and she) may be amazed by a dry bottom level and a dried-out bed each morning.

How to Help Your Toddler Stay Dry

While you need to focus on nighttime dryness when your child reaches the toilet training age, you might help a child who would like to stay dry during the night by doing the following:

- Encourage sufficient daytime liquids, and limit liquids for a couple of hours before bedtime. You don't have to cut out juices completely, because this reduces the quantity of nighttime urine, it generally does not stop the reason for bed-wetting.

- Make several outings to the toilet before bed-time one at the start of your bedtime routine and again at the end, right before lights out. Make sure your son or daughter finishes emptying his or her bladder by calming on the toilet for 3 to 5 moments. An egg timer might help your child understand how long to sit. You will keep him, or her organized with chat, reading a book, or tell a tale. Make this an essential component of your bedtime program.

- Help to make sure that your son or daughter uses the potty frequently during the day, about every single two hours. This encourages regular bladder function and may help with nighttime dryness.

- Direct your son or daughter to utilize the bathroom, whether it's been two hours or if you see symptoms of the need, such as squirming, wiggling, crotch keeping, or dancing.

- Avoid providing any meals or drinks that become stimulants, such as for example, chocolate, sugars, and caffeine, particularly in the hours before bedtime.

- Avoid having your son or daughter wear diapers or absorbent pull-up to bed and make use of a particular mattress cover. Instead, absorbent jeans or diapers will often delay the standard development process just because a kid can't experience when urination happens, and it could also provide him a subconscious message that it is OK to urinate during bedtime because he's putting on his pull-up.

- Make use of positive reinforcement with a sticker chart to help your son or daughter monitor his or her success.

- Keep a night-light-ON, to make the way to the toilet well lit and present your son or daughter access to utilize the toilet at nighttime if he or she must. Simply the subconscious message can help.

- Avoid putting any blame on your child, and don't make him feel guilty or ashamed. Tell him that wetting while asleep is normal and can remember to change.

When to Seek Medical Help?

Based on the National Kidney Foundation, you only need to speak to a doctor about bed-wetting if your son or daughter is 6 to 7 years or older or if presently there are various other symptoms of a sleep problem (such as restless sleep or snoring). However, if your son or daughter is younger than six, but bed-wetting is leading to either her or you distressed, or if you both have daytime toilet complications, you should discuss your concerns with your pediatrician or another professional.

Many small children who are dried out during the night for a lengthy time period start to wet the bed again. That is sometimes due to stress or a period of change within their life, or occasionally because of a medical reason, like a bladder or kidney illness. If your son or daughter suddenly has a switch in her nighttime or daytime bladder or bowel behaviors, it's wise to check with your health treatment provider to ensure he or she doesn't have contamination or another ailment.

With children for whom bed-wetting is a problem, help is a telephone call away. A professional will help you resolve the problem with the use of a bed alarm, bladder training exercises, diet adjustments, therapy, or medicine.

You can contact your doctor for a recommendation.

Why Never to Worry!

There are lots of things we parents must worry about and strive to switch, but usually, during the toddler and preschooler years, bed-wetting isn't among those things. *All you need to do is show patience.* In time it is rather likely your son or daughter will be dry during the night without needing to be included in a remedy at all. And if your son or daughter continues to wet the bed after kindergarten, understand that it isn't his or her fault, and it could be solved respectfully by consulting a professional.

CHAPTER 10

Do's & Don'ts of Potty Training

Don'ts of Potty Training

- Do not get angry. Don't scold your son or daughter or make him or her experience guilt or shame. Your baby isn't doing this deliberately, she isn't attempting to make you mad, and she doesn't know how to resolve this as much as you do.

- Don't make your son or daughter take a seat on the toilet and "try" or push. BMs (bowel motion) happens when your body is prepared and forcing them can make little tears in the anus (fissures) or hemorrhoids, which cause all day discomfort in the rectum. This may cause the child to avoid pooping also may lead to constipation, which creates hard stool, which in turn causes even more hemorrhoids, and on to generate a dreadful routine of discomfort and frustration.

- Don't let your son or daughter stress when he sits to poo. Obviously, a small amount of pushing may be essential for a normal bowel motion. But if he's grunting, straining, and forcing, it's an indicator that either he's probably not set or he's relatively constipated. Have him drink a large glass of drinking water, eat a piece of fruit, and try again in ten or twenty minutes later.

- Don't ever help to make your son or daughter "hold it." When she announces the necessity to go, or if you observe that her body indicators are indicating to go, look for a toilet immediately. Delaying and keeping plays a part in constipation and additional bowel problems.

Do's of Potty Training

- Make certain that your son or daughter is drinking a lot of water the whole day. Stick to drinking water and juice (apple, pear, cranberry, grape, and prune juice however, not orange or various other citrus juices).

- Be sure your son or daughter eats lots of fiber-rich foods each day: vegetables (especially natural ones), fruit, wholegrains, brownish rice, and oatmeal are a few examples. Avoid giving your son or daughter junk food, refined sugar, soda, candy, and chocolate.

- Limit foods that may constipate, such as bananas, rice, apple-sauce, cheese, citrus juice, and carbonated sodas.

- Meals allergies or lactose intolerance (intolerance

to milk products) could cause constipation in a kid. If you suspect this could be true, speak to your doctor.

- If your child shows been constipated, apply petroleum jelly or diaper ointment to her anus before potty appointments.

- Ensure that your child has lots of daily exercise, which stimulates digestion, prevents constipation, and is essential for proper elimination.

- End up being sure that your son or daughter is peeing every hour and two hours. Regular urination can be a necessary element to regular bowel motions.

- Take your son or daughter to the potty first thing in the morning and 10 to 30 mins after a complete meal, when BMs (bowel motion) will probably happen.

- Teach your son or daughter to move when the desire hits. Explain that the poop is wanting to come out and she would need to go to the toilet.

- Purchase a soft, cushioned child's adapter seat for the toilet or a potty chair with a soft seat. Some children find it hard to take a seat on the hard surface area for the amount of time it requires to have a bowel movement.

- If you discover your child has experienced a bowel movement in her slacks, calmly take her to the toilet. Flush her poop straight down the toilet with a comment to clarify that is where it goes. Also get her take a seat on the potty while you wipe her buttocks and let her understand that soon she'll perform her poop on the potty herself.

- If your child is only going to proceed in a diaper, start to have her do thus in the toilet. Progress to making her take a seat on the potty, in her diaper if she'd like. Once she can be used to this, recommend making her diaper off and placing it in to the potty bowl as a "pocket" to capture her poopie.

- You will probably find success by slicing through the crotch of the diaper to ensure that it is still wrapped around her, however the bottom is available to allow poop drop into the potty.

- Help to make sure that your son or daughter sits long enough to empty her bladder or bowel every time she uses the toilet. Make it a soothing 3 to 5 minutes.

- Make certain that your son or daughter's legs are

comfortable, with knees slightly aside and foot firmly planted on the floor or a durable stool.

- Help your child unwind on the potty by reading books, telling a tale, singing a song or listening to one, or chatting.

- Have your son or daughter close her eye and have a few deep breaths while you chat or sing softly.

- Play soothing music during potty sits.

- If your child is showing signs of needing to poop but isn't having the achievement in the toilet, try having him lean ahead and rest his chest muscles against you when you gently rub his lower back. You can also get him sit backward on the toilet and lean against the container.

- Go through books about using the potty, especially those that discuss poop.

CHAPTER 11

Factors that Causes Setbacks during Potty Training

About 80 percent of parent's report suffering toilet training setbacks, therefore you are in extremely good business! There are over a million factors that contribute to kids who are experiencing great achievement with toilet training suddenly move totally backward. Here are some of the more commonly known reasons for setbacks:

- There exists a change in the family members or a disruption in the house, such as relocation, a fresh baby, divorce, marriage, houseguests, or the holiday season.

- The child is uninterested in the toilet training regimen.

- A sickness or damage of the kid or parent

interferes with the most common daily routine for times or weeks.

- There's been a drastic modification in routine, such as starting day treatment, a sibling heading off to college, or an at-home mother or father going off to function.

- The kid has mastered toilet teaching but then has numerous accidents that erode self-confidence. Perhaps an especially embarrassing general public episode takes place, or the unthinking feedback of a member of family or stranger yielding your child experience inadequacy with potty exercise. She may have decided it might be safer if she returned to diapers.

- Your child might have been successful at potty training since you were very successful in reminding him or her to proceed at the proper times. Over time of success you halted reminding him, therefore accidents started to occur.

Setbacks are always temporary; normally, we'd discover second graders putting on diapers. So, whenever a setback occurs with your child, simply set yourself back, right with your kid, and repeat the activities that were effective for you in the past. For instance, if her potty poster was popular, make a fresh one.

Tuck aside your own injured satisfaction, because this has nothing in connection with your task as an instructor nor will it mean your son or daughter has failed potty training. It simply means your son or daughter is normal. Show patience, be supportive, and quickly your baby will be back again to potty success.

Chapter 12

Factors that Warrant Seeing a Doctor

You should contact your wellbeing provider anytime you have concerns on the subject of your child's health. Listed below are a few of the signs that could warrant a telephone call to a doctor:

- Your child hasn't got a bowel motion in four or more days.

- There is bleeding in your child's urine or stool.

- Your child has a fever, is normally nauseous, or is vomiting.

- Your son or daughter isn't urinating every several hours.

- Your son or daughter has problems starting a blast of urine, even when he or she's to pee.

- Your child's urine has a foul smell.

- Your child's belly is protruded, hard, or swollen.

- Your son or daughter's underwear is generally smeared with stool, and it's unrelated to poor wiping practices.

- Your son or daughter is potty qualified but suddenly regresses for no apparent cause.

- You're getting excessively angry over the situation.

Toilet training complications can be quite frustrating and so are one of the significant reasons of child misuse. If you are finding this a great deal to handle, call a reliable friend or a healthcare professional.

If your son or daughter is having difficulty using the toilet, or if toilet training has turned into a main issue in your household, your physician will help you. He or she may analyze the improvement of toilet training, give you advice about diet adjustments, or put your son or daughter on a dietary fiber supplement, stool softener, or moderate laxative, if necessary.

Any child, regardless of how healthy, wise, or able, can have toilet training problems. Any mother or father, no matter how smart or experienced, would want help solving these complications. You shouldn't be shy or embarrassed about seeing a specialist on issues with toilet training. This common, and experts talk to parents each day on this topic.